Ten P[
about [

ex libris

Candlestick Press

Published by:
Candlestick Press,
Diversity House, 72 Nottingham Road, Arnold, Nottingham NG5 6LF
www.candlestickpress.co.uk

Design and typesetting by Craig Twigg

Printed by Bayliss Printing Company Ltd of Worksop, UK

Selection and Introduction © Jessica Mookherjee, 2024

Cover illustration © Clare Curtis
https://clarecurtis.co.uk/

Candlestick Press monogram © Barbara Shaw, 2008

© Candlestick Press, 2024

ISBN 978 1 913627 37 9

Acknowledgements

The poems in this pamphlet are reprinted from the following books, all by
permission of the publishers listed unless stated otherwise. Every effort has been
made to trace the copyright holders of the poems published in this book. The
editor and publisher apologise if any material has been included without
permission, or without the appropriate acknowledgement, and would be glad to
be told of anyone who has not been consulted.

Thanks are due to all the copyright holders cited below for their kind permission.

Kapka Kassabova, *Hwaet! 20 Years of Ledbury Poetry Festival* (Hexham,
Northumberland: Bloodaxe; Ledbury, Hertfordshire: Ledbury Poetry Festival,
2016). Suzannah Evans, *Near Future* (Nine Arches Press, 2018). Andrew
Fusek-Peters, *Mad, Bad and Dangerously Haddock* (Lion Books, 2006) copyright
© Andrew Fusek-Peters 1997, used by permission of the author. Carola Luther,
On the Way to Jerusalem Farm (Carcanet Press, 2021). John McCullough, *Panic
Response* (Penned in the Margins, 2022) by kind permission of the author and
publisher. Jessica Mookherjee, poem first appeared in this pamphlet. Meryl Pugh,
Natural Phenomena (Penned in the Margins, 2018) by kind permission of the
author and publisher. Roger Robinson, *A Portable Paradise* (Peepal Tree Press,
2019). James Tate, *Poetry* (July 1989) and *Distance from Loved Ones* (Wesleyan
University Press, 1990). Courtesy of the Estate of James Tate.

All permissions cleared courtesy of Dr Suzanne Fairless-Aitken –
Swift Permissions swiftpermissions@gmail.com.

Where poets are no longer living, their dates are given.

Introduction

I was brought up in a small coastal town. To me cities were places where dreams could come true, so as soon as possible I moved to London. I found that cities are the sum of all their inhabitants, their stories are the landscape and the show. It's a joy to bring these poems together to illustrate a city's many facets.

Sara Teasdale's poem about New York brings us dreams and lights that link to the ancient cities, where travellers came to see if streets were paved with gold. Those first nights in an unfamiliar city are evoked perfectly in Kapka Kassabova's poem.

There is an 'every city' in these poems. City dwellers know the road everyone hates because of the traffic, amazing flower markets, that secret bakery, the place south of the river where locals never leave, the dangerous places with the best bars... and that place by the river where in certain light you could be on another planet. Suzannah Evans writes of a city taking off into space! These wonder-filled poems make the familiar seem vibrant and strange. Meryl Pugh's city is watery and waking up, Carola Luther's Madrid is full of birds, hearts, shopping and chocolate.

If you allow it, a city becomes a Being made from millions of people. Andrew Fusek-Peter's city is full of emotions. John McCullough's city has no judgements, where it doesn't matter what you are or believe. Roger Robinson's poem gives us a city rising above itself, people holding onto each other, faith needing to exist for the harsh realities of a city. Andrew Tate's city turns us back to the glory of the ordinary, surrounded by lights, a person getting through the day.

Whether you're city dweller or on a city break, I hope you'll find plenty of wonder and love in these *Ten Poems about Cities*.

Jessica Mookherjee

The Lights of New York

The lightning spun your garment for the night
  Of silver filaments with fire shot thru,
  A broidery of lamps that lit for you
The steadfast splendor of enduring light.
The moon drifts dimly in the heaven's height,
  Watching with wonder how the earth she knew
  That lay so long wrapped deep in dark and dew,
Should wear upon her breast a star so white.
The festivals of Babylon were dark
  With flaring flambeaux that the wind blew down;
The Saturnalia were a wild boy's lark
  With rain-quenched torches dripping thru the town –
But you have found a god and filched from him
A fire that neither wind nor rain can dim.

Sara Teasdale

It's Always Strange to Sleep in Cities

It's always strange to sleep in cities
you haven't seen in daylight.
You could be anywhere, anybody
could be breathing next door. In the night
under used blankets you dream
of waking to the highest spires,
fastest clouds, brightest snow.

You dream of drunken rooftops
strewn with broken stars
and you dream of some people you've known.
They're here in the streets,
on the rooftops, in the windows
of the city which is – you awake to find –
nothing but shadows and fog.

It seems they've always been here.
And you tell them without words
because words are not
in the nature of this dream
how happy you are to be here,
How alone, unsure
of the future, of the past.

They thank you for your visit,
everything is fine, they say,
their mouths opening without a voice,
they hope to see you again.
But they don't touch you. Then dawn
breaks over the city
where it is always strange to sleep.

Kapka Kassabova

The Fragile

Between moored hulls that knock together,
A cormorant diving. It surfaces, flips under,
surfaces again. The opaque water
slaps the dockside, hides the cable ends.

Meanwhile, the city wakes up: car horn, shop shutters.
The children devise their Knock-Down Ginger, their Bulrush.
They grin in the street at anyone. Around them
the buildings fade out, rising from shadow to nothing.

Meryl Pugh

Prayer for a Godless City

Air, on earth as you are in heaven, please nurse
our converted churches. Granite gargoyles
cling on over hipster offices. Our angel statue is trapped
in hallucination, its back turned tp rapacious sea.

The pews here are benches for the frayed and sundered
who believe in nothing they cannot clutch or smell
like warm dogs, Frosty Jack's, gnawed chicken legs
forsaken in doorways where death whispers.

Bless us, air, we who linger, exposed to wide open space
where you lunge after roaming the Atlantic
with your cargo of salt, dust and recycled breath,
unbalancing the crowns of elms not far from shore.

Keep slamming into our faces, coursing down
the windpipes of stoners who kite hazily above their legs,
who kneel in bushes on cruising grounds
while you give yourself without judgment

to council estates where the glows of lone cigarettes
at nights are souls drifting; to each corner beneath bridges
where trolleys congregate, buskers cry; to the flat
where a woman rises from under bathwater, gasping.

John McCullough

The Floating City

We got away in the early hours, split the difference
half way across the shopping-centre car park.
We heard the creak of land goodbye-ing land
above the air conditioning of pre-work gyms

as we ran and cycled from no place to another.
Signals switched just in time. Trains nosed
end to end along the station platform. The ocean
sprang out before us like a pop-up tent.

We travelled rudderless with a following wind
trailing power lines and manhole-ladders.
To Scandinavia! Announced the Master Navigator.
We googled the attractions. From the top

of Cemetery Hill we watched whales, each one
its own land-mass. The motorway was nothing
but a frayed edge. The Chief Cartographer
placed a long-distance call for more blue.

Suzannah Evans

The Missing

As if their bodies became lighter,
ten of those seated
in front pews began to float,
and then to lie down as if on
a bed. Then pass down the aisle,
as if on a conveyor belt of pure air,
slow as a funeral cortege,
past the congregants, some sinking
to their knees in prayer.
One woman, rocking back and forth,
muttered, *What about me Lord,*
why not me?

The Risen stream slowly, so slowly
out the gothic doors
and up to the sky, finches darting
deftly between them.

Ten streets away,
a husband tries to hold onto the feet
of his floating wife. At times her force
lifts him slightly off the ground,
his grip slipping. He falls
to his knees with just her high-
heeled shoe in his hand.
He shields and squints his eyes
as she is backlit by the sun.

A hundred people start floating
from the windows of a tower block;
from far enough away they could be
black smoke from spreading flames.

A father with his child on top his shoulders;
men in sandcoloured galiibeas; a woman
with an Elvis quiff and vintage glasses,
a deep indigo hijab flapping in the wind;
an artist in a wax-cloth headwrap:
all airborne, these superheroes,
this airborne pageantry of faith,
this flock of believers.

Amongst the cirrus clouds, floating like hair,
they begin to look like a separate city.
Someone looking on could mistake them
for new arrivants to earth.
They are the city of the missing.
We, now, the city of the stayed.

Roger Robinson

Commerce, Madrid, 2012

All afternoon the geese fly over the city. Women
in twos, waiting for men beside municipal trees.
Shopping continues. The sore sweet
rut of it. We watch traffic, like tourists.

All afternoon the geese fly west over the city, hauling
wakes behind them in strings and waves. Women
stand, disappear, emerge. It's cold. Under glass
we hold hot Spanish chocolate. Shopping continues.

All afternoon labouring geese fly over the city. Cars hoot,
sirens fugue. Beneath bank towers, a statue shifts. A man,
blue clown, blows two-note whistles for a living.
Shopping continues. New women arrive. Others stay

and stay. Geese heave their huge hearts over the city,
the sky a stitched membrane that will hold for a day.
We watch the day end, blood orange. Men come, women
return. Shopping continues. Under lit trees, women in twos.

Carola Luther

Last Night, I Saw the City Breathing

Last night, I saw the city breathing
Great gusts of people,
Rushing in and
Puffing out
Of stations' singing mouths.

Last night, I saw the city laughing.
Takeaways got the giggles,
Cinemas split their sides,
And living rooms completely creased themselves!

Last night, I saw the city dancing.
Shadows were cheek to cheek with brick walls,
Trains wiggled their hips all over the place,
And the trees
In the breeze
Put on a show for an audience of windows!

Last night, I saw the city starving.
Snaking avenue smacked her lips
And swallowed seven roundabouts!
Fat office blocks got stuffed with light
And gloated over empty parking lots.

Last night, I saw the city crying.
Cracked windows poured falling stars
And the streets were paved with mirrors.

Last night, I saw the city sleeping.
Roads night-dreamed,
Street lamps quietly boasted,
'When I grow up, I'm going to be a star!'

And the wind,
Like a cat,
Snoozed in the nooks of roofs.

Andrew Fusek-Peters

The Show

Outside the theatre, a family from Brixton sit by a river that washes
against concrete. Food stalls blow fennel, cumin, salt-fish. Home

at the back of throats. A mile away barbershops open. As the sun sets
men get hair cuts, three girls shout at cab drivers, hold each other in heels,

stumble as stains leak from threads. Outside the theatre,
strangers talk *white flight*, *black flight*, house prices, life in the nineties.

The child's just learnt about this in her geography class, the rest
nod, eat curry with thin-wooden forks. Eyes, the colour of London river,

hold a promise of flood. Her father; brings donuts, answers the *where are you*
from? with *Serbia but born here* says his grandfather was caught up in a war

in the nineties, her mother tells a tiny woman who takes no space at the table,
of her arrival from Mauritius when she was five, now scents around her are

things she can't quite remember. And a mile away a cab passes Power
Church, internet café, signs for English classes, beauty places where women

tut and nod, men mumble about business. Outside the theatre a tiny white
woman says her mother sent her from Hackney to Cornwall to escape

bombs in the forties. A mile away on the corner of Wyndem Road a cab stops
for a stranger, drives her east to Tilbury. There the river opens to a vast

world, filled with such brightness; laps at the merging, glinting silt platelets,
tastes the world's stories far from the city's brick-dust fever dream.

Jessica Mookherjee

City at Night

The blue-black plumes of the fountain
parched my yearning, and a tuft of cellophane
clings fondly to my foot like a diadem.
Down that street an uproar is dwindling,
a small word had been magnified and was
once again shrinking back to its reasonable size,
and Joe Blow drifts down to the riverbank
searching for relics, a man of sorrows.
Then a new turmoil infects another flock,
it's a good corner on which to sell balm.
A seer bobs along, oblivious or beguiled.
I look for my reflection in a window:
Goodnight Joe, Goodnight Joe, Goodnight.

James Tate